SUFFERING
In Silence

Dr. Milicent J.Coburn

Order this book online at www.trafford.com
or email orders@trafford.com

Most Trafford titles are also available at major online book retailers.

Scripture taken from The Holy Bible, King James Version. Public Domain

Print information available on the last page.

ISBN: 978-1-6987-0787-7 (sc)
ISBN: 978-1-6987-0788-4 (e)

Trafford rev. 06/17/2021

Trafford
PUBLISHING®   www.trafford.com
North America & international
toll-free: 844-688-6899 (USA & Canada)
fax: 812 355 4082

CONTENTS

DEDICATION

This book is dedicated to all those who have suffered some abuse or other. Those whose hurt take time to heal.

INTRODUCTION
Suffering in Silence

Suffering in silence is not a matter of why? But when? Almost everyone at some time or other has an experience or experiences where he or she cannot say anything as situations arise. Yes, there are some strong-willed persons who will always be combative, and so they do not take the sitting position. They fight to the end, win or lose. There are folks who are in the wrong, but they do not back off.

The rest of us give up our rights for fear sometimes, yes, I say fear. The others of us surrender because it will bring some peace in the situation. It may not solve the problem, but it prevents the problem from exploding. It may give a wrong impression, that we are silly, weak, afraid, cornered or that we may have lost the fight. When I was younger, I heard my parents speaking about, "a still tongue keeps a cool head." There are situations in which we just sit and assess everything.

Then again, there are circumstances where people are physically threatened. Their families or themselves would suffer and even be killed, so they are told to keep the matter quiet. It is as if one becomes a human pressure cooker that is steaming on the inside and there is no outlet, because of fear. This fear is legitimate because one has seen or experience the outcome of similar situations when they escalate.

What is the alternative to suffering in silence? Is there a resolution? How can one person continue living a healthy meaningful life with so much heaviness, stress, fear and weight on the inside?

The family is the nucleus of society, if the family disintegrates then the nation is in a downward spiral. We observe more and more families being destroyed by domestic violence, and this is by family members who cause it and very few strangers. We send our military members to war, but the war is in the homes and nothing is being done to heal or counteract it. Family members suffer in silence and by the time someone who is outside discovers it, it is far too late. The "scrambled egg" cannot be placed together again. It is no different from Humpty Dumpty falling off the wall and cannot be put back together again. I really feel the hurt for all the abused especially the innocent children. May God help us all.

ABRAHAM

• • • • • • • • • ● ○○○○○○○○○ ○ ○

God called Abram in a very unique way. The Lord told Abram:

> "Leave your country, your relatives, and your father's house, and go to the land that I will show you. I will cause you to become the father of a great nation. I will bless you and make you famous, and I will make you a blessing to others. I will bless those who bless you and curse those who curse you. All the families of the earth will be blessed through you." (Genesis 12:1-3)

Abram did not question God, he made ready for his departure. Abram being an unselfish man invited his nephew Lot, to accompany him and his immediate household. God's covenant did not include Lot, neither did God make a covenant with Lot, so he was just piggy backing on Abram's good side. You may not be aware of the fact that Lot's father, Haran had died at a very young age therefore Abram was an adopted father to Lot.

Abram was very wealthy and also was Lot and that is quite understandable. As they journeyed, Abram built an altar and worshipped God. There is no record of Lot worshipping. Lot was capturing the picturesque landscape. An argument developed between the herdsmen of Abram and the herdsmen of Lot. These men were contending for the best pasture lands that they deemed best for their herd. Like a good natured and considerate father, Abram discovered the problem with the workers, called Lot and discussed his observation. He reminded Lot that they were brothers and should live peaceably, especially amongst the ungodly neighbors. He then gave Lot the opportunity to choose the portion of land that he wanted to occupy, and he Abram would be content with what remained.

Lot observed the fertile plains with luscious grasslands, and did not give it a second thought, he took those grasslands. He never thought of asking his uncle if he would take the first choice. The wonderful grasslands of Sodom were well watered, and he was cognizant that his livestock would flourish in that area, and he would be wealthier than his uncle. How-be-it Abram did not object to his choice, he kept his dignity because he believed God, and was following His lead.

Abram remained in Canaan while Lot remained in the Jordan Valley to the east of them, very close to Sodom before the Lord destroyed it. Lot was very comfortable, but God appeared to Abram and informed him that he should just look as far as he could see, and that possession would be his, and his descendants, who would be like the dust of the earth, that is impossible to be numbered. Lot was proud of his assets, but of course God did not include him in His plans or preferably, His covenant with Abram. Abram did not complain about Lot's treatment meted out to him but instead he kept silent. Lot did not know this quote, "You can be sure that your sin will track you down." (Number 32:23b).

Lot was so complacent when suddenly, a war broke out in the area. Four kings attacked the king of Sodom and others of his associates, at least five kings in all. Lot was captured and all his goods were taken. One of the men escaped and informed Abram, who took 318 of the men of his household and rescued Lot and his effects from Chedorlaomer's army. Abram could have said that Lot got what he deserved, but instead he restored him. He could have given him a good lecture for the future, but he lived to please God. Lot probably did not appreciate his uncle before but when he received his possessions, all his women, and other captives, he must have thought differently. Uncle Abram was a liberator in the true sense of the word

Abram was Lot's parent since his father's demise at an early age. When Lot was captured in Sodom, Abram could have allowed him to" learn his lesson" as we would say nowadays. Abram did not have to bring back Lot, his family, and possessions out of captivity, but he recovered them. Lot was a very selfish young man who was concerned about himself. I doubt that he thanked Abram. Because Abram was a "Friend of God" and was living by faith he could not treat Lot as he deserved. I thank God because He does not treat us as we deserve. God's love is unfathomable. Abram had a heart like God's.

Lot reminds me of the story of The Prodigal Son who requested of his father, his possession. His father was still alive and he knew that one day his father would bestow on him his rightful share but he could not wait. His father presented him with his portion of the goods, and the boy moved away from home immediately. The son lived like a millionaire until he lost everything. One day he came to his senses and decided to return home. When he got home looking, dirty, disheveled and empty handed, his father received him and threw a party for him. Like the Prodigal Son, I hope that Lot had learnt his lesson, to be kind to everyone especially your parent(s) because some day you may need them.

ABRAM AND ISAAC

bram and the Lord had a discourse in which Abram explained that he had no heir, so his servant Eliezer's son would inherit his possession. The Lord explained to Abram that his servant's son would never be his heir. In order to substantiate the argument, the Lord took Abram outside and instructed him to look up in the night's sky and count the stars. Well of course, that was an impossible act. The Lord stated that his descendants would be like that, impossible to count and they would receive his wealth.

One day Sarai, Abram's wife encouraged him to go to bed with her Egyptian maid, Hagar. Abram slept with Hagar to please Sarai and she conceived and bore a son to Abram. Hagar was the first surrogate mom. Hagar began to "pop style" on her mistress because she was able to give her husband a son when he could not get one otherwise.

God appeared to Abram when he was ninety-nine years old. He changed his name to Abraham and established a covenant with him, saying that he would make him a mighty nation.

> "This is my covenant with you: I will make you the father of not just one nation, but a multitude of nations! What's more, I am changing your name. It will no longer be Abram; now you will be known as Abraham, for you will be the father of many nations. I will give you millions of descendants who will represent many nations. Kings will be among them!
>
> I will continue this everlasting covenant between us, generation after generation. It will continue between me and your offspring forever. And I will always be your God and the God of your descendants after you. Yes, I will give all this land of Canaan to you and to your offspring forever. And I will be their God." (Genesis 17:4-6)

God revealed to Sarai, now Sarah (meaning mother of many nations) that she would have a son. She had heard the conversation between Abraham and the Lord. She was in a state of shock, so she laughed because she was too old to bear a child. A man at the age of 100 years old and his wife 90 are not the candidates for a baby, "With God nothing is impossible." Just as God had promised, Abraham and Sarah had a son and named him Isaac, meaning "Laughter" because Sarah had laughed.

Years later God tested Abraham's faith and obedience. "Abraham!" God called. "Yes," he replied. "Here I am." Take your son, your only son – yes, Isaac, whom you love so much – and go to the land of Moriah. Sacrifice him there as a burnt offering on one of the mountains, which I will point out to you." (Genesis 22:16). Abraham couldn't tell Sarah because she would think that a 100 plus year old man is somewhat crazy. Sarah waited so long to have a child and now it would kill her to lose him. What would the neighbors say? How could Abraham inform her of such a story?

One would think that Abraham was joyous when he made ready the things he needed for his journey the next morning. He had to be obedient to God and yet he had what felt like a stone in his chest.

Did God really want me to kill my only son after waiting so long for him? You may ask if he did not have Ishmael, yes but that child was not the child of promise. He was like a one-night-stand son. God did not promise Abraham Ishmael, that child was "cooked up" between him and Sarah. As he, his son Isaac, and the servants travelled, Abraham was wondering if he had really heard God say that he should sacrifice Isaac. Some of us present day, Christians would curse the devil and cast him out when God is instructing us to do something some what strange or difficult. There are many Christians who would begin to speak in tongues and blame the devil. To be honest it couldn't be God instructing his servant and friend to take his only son and offer him up as a sacrifice. After waiting 100 years for the promised child he should offer him up. It must have been a dream. He had probably eaten something the previous night that caused him to have a nightmare. He heard of people having weird dreams but, not him, especially this one. What will Sarah think? He must have wondered if he was losing his mind, or that he had that new illness Alzheimer. The fact still remained, God had instructed him to give up Isaac, the" Son of Promise." Abram was determined to obey no matter the outcome. We accuse the devil of everything whether good or bad, there is nothing good about him, and he has no alibi.

Abraham suffered in silence all the way up the mountain. As he neared the spot where he should offer up his only son, his heart became heavy and he was waiting for God to say something different. He informed his servants to remain at a certain spot while he and his son go further to worship and return. Was his heart really saying return? He trusted God. Isaac then broke the silence; "Father?" His father answered. "Yes, my son," "We have the wood and the fire," said the boy, "but where is the lamb for the sacrifice?" (Genesis 22:6c – 7)

Abraham explained that God will provide the lamb. As they got to the spot, Abraham placed the wood, then Isaac on top. He took out the knife with the intention of a quick blow so the lad would not suffer, and he would not observe the pain that he had caused his son to bear. He heard the angel of the Lord calling.

> "At that moment the angle of the Lord shouted to him from heaven, "Abraham! Abraham!"
>
> "Yes," he answered. "I'm listening" "Lay down the knife," the angel said.

"Do not hurt the boy in any way, for now I know that you truly fear God. You have not withheld even your beloved son from me." (Genesis 22:11-12)

Abraham saw a ram caught in the thicket for the sacrifice. He could not audibly explain how he had felt since the Lord instructed him to offer up his son. Abram was so relieved to have his son alive,

JOSEPH

Joseph's story is a very unique one, in that his dad Jacob, was sent to Haran by Isaac his father to prevent a possible murder between his two sons Esau and Jacob. Jacob met his uncle Laban who had two daughters, the older Leah and the younger Rachael. Leah was not attractive. She had a problem with her eyes. They were probably looking in opposite direction. She should have used very dark sunglasses when she was of engagement years. Leah didn't know how to conceal blemishes from the public as we do now a days. Rachael was beautiful and caused a man's heart to get double beats because she was so gorgeous.

Jacob had asked his uncle Laban for the hand of Rachael in marriage, he was given a woman to sleep with overnight, but when daylight came, he discovered that he was tricked. Instead of going to bed with Rachael, he slept with Leah whom he disliked.

He had worked seven years for the first dowry, now to get Rachael also he had to work another seven years. Jacob questioned his uncle, now father-in-law of the switch-trick and was given this reply: "It is not the custom in our country, "Laban replied, "to marry off a younger daughter before an older one." (Genesis 29:26) Jacob forgot the trick that he had played on his father, Isaac. One day his father felt like eating delectable meal, so he called his older son and requested a meal that he alone could prepare. The boys mother heard the conversation and hastily called Jacob and told him of his father's request.

Jacob was a mommy's boy who remained in the house; while Esau was a hunter and the father's favorite. Rebecca instructed Jacob to fetch a young goat for her to prepare. Jacob reminded his mother that his brother was hairy while he was smooth. She told him that she was in charge of that. problem. Please take into consideration that Dad had lost his sight. Rebecca placed the dead kid's skin over Jacob's arm so that he felt hairy and smell like a goat. He took the meal to his father who asked him how he returned so soon, and he lied that God had provided. Isaac informed him that his voice sounded like Jacob's. Dad then called him closer and felt the hairy skin. The imposter, Jacob thought he had gotten away with his trick, but suddenly Esau walked in and heard his father pronouncing the blessing on Jacob thinking it was Esau. Jacob had to leave home or else Esau would have killed him. Jacob landed in his uncle's hands where he was being tricked.

Leah's soil was very fertile, so it did not take long for her to produce babies, one after the other, while Rachael was barren. One day Rachael confronted Jacob because of her unfruitfulness.

> "Now when Rachael saw that she bear Jacob no children, Rachael envied her sister, and said to Jacob, "Give me children, or else I die!" and Jacob's anger was aroused against Rachael, and he said "Am I in the place of God, who has withheld from you the fruit of the womb?" (Genesis 3:1-2)

When it is God's time, he takes care of his created ones, so he remembered Rachael and she conceived and bore a son, and named him, Joseph, because "God has taken away my reproach." Jacob, his family and his possessions returned home after twenty years.

Jacob preferred Joseph over his eleven brothers which resulted in a family rift. Joseph's brothers hated him and that was expected especially since his father

Jacob endowed him with a coat of many colors. God blessed Joseph with dreams that caused his siblings to treat him as an outsider, an outcast, a misfit, a black sheep, a sore thumb and saw him as very pretentious. Joseph would sometimes report to his father of the evil deeds of his older brothers, which caused them to despise him the more. Jacob believed any report Joseph gave him and that was certainly asking for trouble if his beautiful coat and his dreams were insufficient trouble.

One day Joseph was sent by his dad to check up on his brothers in the field and they seized the opportunity to destroy him and his dreams. They were determined to kill him, but Reuben, one of them saw a pit and requested that he be thrown in it, instead. He had planned to go behind the backs of the other ten brothers and rescue Joseph. In Reuben's absence the other ten brothers took Joseph out of the pit and sold him to some Ishmaelite traders who were in transit. Joseph was subsequently sold again, this time to Potiphar, an officer of Pharaoh, king of Egypt. The brothers schemed up to deceive their father by killing a kid, dipping the coat of many colors in its blood, and informed their dad that the coat was found in the field. Jacob concluded that a wild animal had destroyed Joseph. Since that revelation, conclusion, and belief,

Jacob couldn't be comforted, because Joseph was the child of his old age.

While Joseph was in Egypt, he was elevated to a prominent position in Potiphar's household. Potiphar was confident that Joseph could be the administrator over his entire possession, except for his wife of course. God was with Joseph and blessed everything that he did.

Joseph was young, handsome and of great stature, so his master's wife began to lust after him. Whenever that foxy woman's eyes beheld Joseph she salivated and schemed how to seduce him. This old goat of a woman is what we call a robber of the cradle. She had a lustful eye on this young man. She observed him daily as he managed the affairs that were entrusted to him.

One day she cornered Joseph and demanded that he go to bed with her, but he rejected her. And remarked:

> "Look, he told her, my master trusts me with everything in his entire household. No one here has more authority than I do! He has held back nothing from me except you, because you are his wife. How could I ever do such a wicked thing? It would be a great sin against God." (Genesis 39:8-9)

It so happened that Mrs. Potiphar kept pursuing Joseph day after day, until, finally, they were alone in the house and the pervert, predator, dream killer, rapist, grabbed his cloak and he released it, and ran for his life. She began to broadcast it that her husband brought Joseph in her home and he attempted to rape her, and she had the evidence to substantiate it. Can this be true? Mrs. Potiphar screamed and cried crocodile tears. She could not give her husband a chance to get in the house when she began to complain about Joseph. She deployed the false, damning story about Joseph. Her husband pleased her by placing Joseph in prison. He trusted Joseph but he had to please his wife by believing her false accusation.

Joseph knew that he was innocent, and God knew also. Joseph suffered in silence. He had no one to comfort him. He was snatched from his loving father, placed in a pit and could have been murdered, sold to traders, and now lies placed him in prison. God was with Joseph and the jailer placed him as supervisor of all the other prisoners.

It was a matter of time when two of Pharaoh's servants were placed in the prison. After a time, the baker and cupbearer both had separate dreams and told them to Joseph who interpreted them both. Joseph requested that the cupbearer remember him to

Pharaoh, just to say a complimentary word for him. The cupbearer was restored as Joseph had said, but he forgot Joseph. "Pharaoh's cup-bearer, however, promptly forgot all about Joseph, never giving him a thought. (Genesis 40:23) Joseph suffered in silence.

Two years later, Pharaoh had dreams and God made it that the cupbearer informed Pharaoh of Joseph who had interpreted his and the baker's dreams.

> "Then the king's cup-bearer spoke up. Today I have been reminded of my failure," he said. "Some time ago, you were angry with the chief baker and me, and you imprisoned us in the palace of the captain of the guard. One night the chief baker and I each had a dream, and each dream had a meaning. We told the dreams to a young Hebrew man who was a servant of the captain of the guard. He told us what each of our dreams meant, and everything happened just as he said it would." (Genesis 41:9-13)

Pharaoh sent for Joseph, had Joseph interpret his dreams. Pharaoh made him ruler over the land of Egypt. There were seven years of famine and Joseph's brothers had to come to Egypt to purchase food. They didn't recognize him because he was now a man, dressed in royal apparel and spoke like the Egyptians. Joseph recognized his brothers and had no ill feelings against them. He did not identify himself because it was not God's time for him to do so.

Joseph was suffering inside, because on one of the occasions when his brothers came for provisions, he retreated to himself and wept bitterly. Joseph had experienced so much pain and his only outlet was to sob by himself without anyone to complain to. Joseph knew how to suffer in silence. When he met his brothers, he could have treated them with revenge, but he was aware that God orchestrated it. In other words, it was all in the plan for his life. His dreams manifested themselves in a mysterious manner, but they were prophetic.

Joseph's brothers tried repeatedly to kill his dreams, but failed. Mrs. Potiphar made a daring attempt to destroy Joseph's dreams, but she only propelled him to greatness. God had Joseph in his providential care and nothing on the outside could destroy him. Joseph was the only one who could railroad his dreams, but because of his integrity he suffered in silence until God rewarded him openly.

TAMAR

• • • • • • • • ● ○○○○○○○○○ ○ ○

One of Jacob's son, Judah, had a daughter-in-law named Tamar. This woman was shrewd to some extent, and rightly so, because someone pushed the wrong button. It was a custom in those days for surviving brothers to marry their widowed sister-in-law and raise up seed for the deceased brother.

Both of Jacob's oldest sons Onan and Er had died because they were wicked. At their death, Shelah the surviving brother, was very young so Judah instructed Tamar to go home to her father and wait for Shelah to mature, but he had deceived her. The trick was that she would have waited all of her life but not for Shelah's hand in marriage. Judah was protecting Shelah from dying like his brothers. He was not certain that Shelah would die, never the less he was not taking a chance with this son.

During the wait, Judah's wife died, and after the mourning was over, he went with a friend to Timnah to supervise the shearing of his sheep. Someone told Tamar that her father-in-law was in the vicinity. Tamar was suffering in silence.

> "Tamar was aware that Shelah had grown up, but they had not called her to come and marry him. So she changed out of her widow's clothing and covered herself with a veil to disguise herself. Then she sat beside the road at the entrance to the village Enaim, which is on the way to Timnah. Judah noticed her as he went by and thought she was a prostitute, since her face was veiled. So he stopped and propositioned her to sleep with him, not realizing that she was his own daughter-in-law." (Genesis 38:14-16)

Judah now fell in a trap that he did not expect. Tamar was pregnant for her father-in-law. He deceived her and now it reverses on him. She had requested some valuable, interesting articles before she slept with him. He was offering her a goat, but her trick was worth far more than a kid. He wanted to sleep with her, so he paid her the price supposing she was a harlot.

When it was revealed to Judah that Tamar was pregnant, he was indignant.

> "About three months later, word reached Judah that Tamar, his daughter-in-law was pregnant as a result of prostitution. "Bring her out and burn her!" Judah shouted.
>
> But as they were taking her out to kill her, she sent this message to her father-in-law: "The man who owns this identification seal and walking stick is the father of my child. Do you recognize them?" (Genesis 38:24-25)

What Judah had done to Tamar was inexcusable. It was incredible when Tamar showed up to be stoned with Judah's trophies. Why are the ladies the ones to be killed? Tamar was pregnant so that would be double murder. It reminds me of the story where the woman caught in adultery was taken to Jesus because she was "caught in the very act." The man was never presented. He might very well be one of them with the stones. It was different in Tamar's case because she had important evidence that belonged to the man who passed the verdict, Judah. He was ashamed of himself and in the end, he thought of her as being more righteous than he. Some women are very dangerous when they suffer in silence, if you don't believe, ask Tamar. Her silent suffering brought out the evil in her father-in-law and proved that not everyone can be trusted.

HANNAH

There was a man by the name of Elkanah, who had two wives. Please don't get any ideas that it's ok to have more than one spouse at any given time. Well, the names of Elkanah's wives were Hannah and Peninnah. Yes, Peninnah had children while Hannah was barren. In my day and time some women would call Hannah a "mule," because she was childless. Peninnah meted out taunts and smart jokes day after day to Hannah. Peninnah was very mean, just like some bullies we may know, she was so cruel. Elkanah loved Hannah and when he offered sacrifice, Hannah got the best portion from him.

> "Year after year it was the same — Peninnah would taunt Hannah as they went to the tabernacle. Hannah would finally be reduced to tears and would not even eat. "What's the matter,

Hannah?" Elkanah would ask. "Why aren't you eating? Why be so sad just because you have no children? You have me — isn't that better than having ten sons?" (I Samuel 1:7-8)

The Lord had closed up Hannah's womb, but Peninnah did not know. Hannah was suffering in silence. She realized that her husband loved her, but she needed to have even one child, and that would make a difference. Hannah had to endure the mocking, jeering and insults of the other woman in the same home. It is one thing to have an enemy on the street, but it is a different thing to be residing under the same roof with her or him. It is unhealthy to share the same living space with someone as cruel as Peninnah, and of course the same husband.

We should take a page out of Hannah's book in that she went to the tabernacle or house of the Lord when all else failed. It sometimes hurts in the church as well. The family was at Shiloh and after the meal, Hannah went to the tabernacle to pray to the Lord. The Priest Eli was sitting in his customary spot beside the entrance, his eyes were then fixed on Hannah who was on the altar.

"Hannah was in deep anguish, crying bitterly as she prayed to the Lord. And she made this vow: "O LORD Almighty, if you will look down upon my sorrow and answer my prayer and give me a son then I will give him back to you. He will be yours for his entire lifetime, and as a sign that he has been dedicated to the LORD, his hair will never be cut.""

As she was praying to the LORD, Eli watched her. Seeing her lips moving but hearing no sound, he thought she had been drinking. "Must you come here drunk?" he demanded. "Throw away your wine!"

"Oh no, sir!" she replied, "I'm not drunk! But I am very sad, and I was praying out my heart to the LORD. Please don't think I am a wicked woman! For I have been praying out of great anguish and sorrow." (I Samuel 1:10-16)

I hope that you understand why I stated that you can be misunderstood and subsequently hurt in the church. The priest's account of her being drunk was wrong, fake news. When others judge you wrongfully, it hurts, but the priest or your spiritual advisor doing it makes it unforgiveable. This can compound the sorrow you are feeling already. God gave Hannah, her baby boy, Samuel, Halleluiah! Samuel excelled all of Peninnah's children, in fact there's no record of them. Hannah gave Samuel to the Lord as she had promised: Samuel, meaning "I asked the LORD for him." She also gave birth to other children after giving birth to Samuel, the prophet, priest and deliverer in Israel. Please laugh all you want now Ms. Peninnah! The person who laughs first in a situation will not be able to laugh in the end. Peninnah laughed herself out of the family. The joke was on her but Hannah the lady, would not laugh at her because she had so much to be grateful for. God made her triumph over the enemy.

I praise the Lord that Peninnah did not know of the encounter with Eli the priest, and Hannah in the Temple. I am certain that she would use that as a curse on Hannah. She would make certain that she stressed the drunken portion of her ridicule, because the priest deemed her a drunken woman. Hannah would be in a worse state than the predicament that she was already experiencing. That wretch Peninnah was an evil woman and I blame Elkanah to have two wives in the same home. As a woman I realize that one is a problem, but to have two wives and one is Peninnah was truly a disaster. Peninnah was neither loving nor kind. She did not have a compassionate nor sympathetic heart. Hannah on the other hand was a wise and caring woman; one who made a promise to God and kept it.

ELIZABETH

Zechariah was a member of the priestly group. His wife was Elizabeth, who was also of the priestly line. "Zechariah and Elizabeth were righteous in God's eyes, careful to obey all the Lord's commandments and regulations." (Luke 1:6) Elizabeth was barren and both Elizabeth and Zechariah were old.

Elizabeth did not complain but she was suffering in silence, because it was a custom in those days for women to have children to be regarded as special ladies to their husbands and to the public. Zechariah was in the sanctuary one day and an angel of the Lord appeared to him and announced that Elizabeth would have a baby, a son to be concise. The angel gave him the name of the baby "John" also directives as to how to care for John because he was not an ordinary baby. John would be used by God to prepare Israel for Jesus' coming.

Zechariah questioned the angel as to how he and his wife would become parents at that old age when women ceased to bear children. The angel identified himself as Gabriel, who stands in God's presence, so Zechariah did not require any other validation.

> "He stayed at the Temple until his term of service was over, and then he returned home. Soon afterward, his wife, Elizabeth, became pregnant and went into seclusion for five months. "How kind the Lord is!" she exclaimed. "He has taken away my disgrace of having no children!" (Luke 1:23-25)

Because Zachariah doubted God, he was dumb for the duration of Elizabeth's pregnancy After the time appointed, Elizabeth gave birth to John and it brought joy to her neighbors and relatives. Everyone informed her that the baby should not be called John because no one in their family had that name. Prior to her giving birth that was not taken into consideration: now that she has given birth they had an objection to the name she gave her child. They then questioned Zachariah about the name given and he took a tablet and wrote, "John" After he had confirmed the name his speech was restored. The Lord was kind to her to give her a child in her old age. God knows how to bring joy to those who are sad and heavy laden. An old woman and her old husband now embrace a baby, and a very special one at that. Elizabeth was no more the talk of the town in a negative way but a positive one. Elizabeth had no reason to be silent or in obscurity because she delivered a baby who is the forerunner of Jesus. He led people to repentance before Jesus' Ministry began.

MARY JESUS' MOTHER

Mary, a young virgin girl was engaged to Joseph a carpenter, then one day she had a very special visit from an angel. The angel Gabriel arrived with a fascinating message. Mary would become pregnant and bring forth a son and His name would be called Jesus. Gabriel gave Mary every detail of the child that she should know. But Mary's question was, "How could that be seeing she was a virgin." The angel explained the Immaculate Conception Birth to her.

It was not easy for Mary to explain how she became pregnant and her intended husband had had no intercourse with her. Joseph was distraught and decided to divorce her privately, but the angel calmed his fears in a dream, and informed him of Mary's pregnancy and instructed him that he was not to divorce her. Mary had to travel around with her pregnancy. Thank God that the men in that vicinity didn't bring her in the public to be stoned. The other women who knew that she was not married talked about her. She was the gossip of the town. Mary finally left town to visit her cousin Elizabeth in the hill country of Judea.

Mary was able to escape the eyes of the ladies in Galilee. For the first time she departed from their scrutiny and judgmental talk. For the first time Mary was celebrated, because the baby in her cousin Elizabeth's womb leaped as she entered the house. Elizabeth and Mary were able to rejoice in the Lord.

At last Mary brought forth her wonderful Baby. Then Mary, Joseph and Baby Jesus (family) had a visitation from some shepherds.

> "Now when they had seen Him, they made widely known the saying which was told them concerning this Child.
>
> And all those who heard it marveled at those things which were told them by the shepherds. But Mary kept all these things and pondered them in her heart." (Luke 2:17-19)

It so happened that it was time to present the baby, to the Lord, there was a devout servant in the temple by the name of Simeon and he was waiting for the Messiah. The Holy Spirit had informed him that death would wait until he saw the Messiah. The very day Mary and Joseph arrived with Baby Jesus, in the Temple, the Holy Spirit moved on Simeon. As soon as he saw the Baby, Simeon began to glorify God.

> "Jesus' parents were amazed at what was being said about him. Then Simeon, blessed them, and he said to Mary, the baby's mother, "This child is destined to cause many in Israel to fall, but he will be a joy to many others. He has been sent as a sign from God, but many will oppose him. As a result, the deepest thoughts of many hearts will be revealed. And a sword will pierce your very soul." (Luke 2:33-35)

At the end of Jesus' ministry when he was arrested and beaten, Mary was suffering in silence. She stood at the foot of the cross at the crucifixion and her heart ached. Jesus himself instructed the disciple who loved Him and whom He loved to care for her.

THE HOME

••••••••●○○○○○○○○○○

"Jesus knew their thoughts and replied, "Any kingdom that wars with itself is doomed. A city or home divided against itself is doomed."" (Matthew 12:25). The scripture here is addressing division in the home. There is sometimes more violence in the home than anywhere else. As we grapple with tragic and difficult circumstances in homes, we need to take notice of the reminder in the Bible.

> "History merely repeats itself. It has all been done before. Nothing under the sun is truly new. What can you point to that is new? How do you know it didn't already exist long ago? We don't remember what happened in those former times. And in future generations, no one will remember what we are doing now." (Ecclesiastes 1:9–11)

How can someone understand cases where fathers rape their own infants, some have died as a result of the injuries that they received. These babies literally suffer in silence never to speak before or after the cruelty had taken place. There were two,(I am certain that there are thousands that have not been reported,) event where the father raped all his girls and had babies with them in their own homes. We sometimes wonder if no neighbor noticed anything, just a slight inkling to do a little investigation. Where are the mothers of these children who are being abused? Are they also victims or are they afraid, or just turned a blind eye to the situation?

I have watched cases where the wife or girlfriend stated that the man caused her to cut ties with her friends and family. He then abuses her because she was naive and alone. She did not see the problems ahead in that he took control over her life after isolating her. She suffers in silence. There are many domestic violence victims who suffer in silence to the point of being murdered and unfortunately babies and other children are not exempt. I know that there are men who suffer from domestic violence, and in some cases, they do not disclose the abuse to friends and family members, because of the negative stigma in our society; men don't cry, and men are strong. Yet men are carriers of physical, emotional and social scars.

I heard of a story some time ago of some young girls who were orphans and they resided with their grandmother and uncle. The grandmother was always inebriated. The uncle raped all the girls, threatened them with a knife to keep them quiet. The people around him were afraid of him. There was another case where both parents died when the child was seven years old. She had to reside with her father's brother and his wife. The aunt abused the child repeatedly and there was no one to defend her. It got so grotesque that at fifteen years of age her father's brother began to sexually assault her. Suffering in silence is very painful.

Many years ago, a former classmate of mine who was in her early twenties informed me that that afternoon she was going to leave home. Her husband knew when she should get home. He knew the mileage that should be on the speedo meter. He checked on her. She had planned a way to escape that afternoon. I do not know if she had carried out her plan.

Little children are great at keeping secrets. When they are threatened by adults and older individuals. They keep quiet and they withdraw. They do not act like they should as normal children, they have a burden on their little shoulders. There are a few children especially girls who disclose information to their mothers who blame them for what occurs(ed). Other mothers accuse their girls of lying. Needless to say, these sexually abused children have no one to defend them. Recently a teenage girl was raped and killed by her uncle who gave some fictitious account, but the courts did not believe him. We have heard of stories where parents set up cameras in their homes and on occasions they catch the caregiver abusing their children. These children are unable to explain the suffering that they are enduring, but the cameras speak for them. There are some baby-sitters who sexually abuse children as well.

The Scripture always has a kind, compassionate word about children. These verses state it well.

"Don't you see that children are God's best gift?

The fruit of the womb, his generous legacy.

Like warrior's fistful of arrows are the children of a vigorous youth.

Oh, how blessed are you parents, with your quivers full of children!

Your enemies don't stand a chance against you, you'll sweep them right off your doorstep." (Psalm 127:3-5)

Our children need special care so they can be the people God intends them to be. Some of the stories we read are horrible, but nonetheless, I think they will encourage us to protect children. We grow up hearing that it takes a village to grow children, but where is the village when the need is there? Many years ago, my class required me to go to the courthouse and review some cases. One case that caught my attention had a little girl between the ages of three and four whose mother was always dressed up and ready to roam the streets at nights. The father was standing there speechless while the little daughter pleaded with her mom to stay home, who never acquiesced.

As soon as the mother left the home he went in the child's room and began to molest her. I later watched the movie of the same case where he called out to the child with his beer in his hand. On one occasion, he pushed the door and the child just looked with wide eyes as he entered. I think that that was so disgusting, it was more than incest, it was rape, by a father. The little girl had no deliverance, no protection, and no help. In another case the mother's boyfriend started to rape the child at six years old. She was afraid to inform her mother because her younger siblings' father had left and she did not want to be the reason why this one leaves. At the age of 13 he suggested that her mother send her to reside with her father. Soon after she left the man left her mother. She subsequently tell her mom who was sorry that it took place. She was finally taken to the doctor but there was no evidence because it happened too long ago.

I just read a case where the mother allowed the stepbrother to rape the 11-year-old daughter repeatedly. She did nothing to stop it. He even performed other sexual acts on this child. The mother was sentenced to six months in jail or a few thousand dollars (not in U.S.A) of course. The people in the community were perturbed because of the light sentence. and passed their own sentence. Some of them stated that if she were residing in another community she would pay dearly for the crime. One young lady stated to the news reporter that when she was a young girl a younger next-door neighbor confided to her that her mother allowed a taxi man to have sex with her at nights for money. The young lady who was then reporting it said that she herself was young and did not know what to do regarding the report.

Children suffer in silence because some of them cannot verbalize what they experience, others are threatened with physical violence even death. When a child discloses certain information to her teacher, it is reported to the proper channel but in the final analysis the mother states that the child lied. The child is looked upon as someone who is untrustworthy. The future of that child looks bleak unless there is an advocate. A trustful person gives reliable guidance to the abused. God speaks kindly of children in His word.

One of our popular newspapers had a caption on January 26, 2020:- "Parenting? Mandatory Classes Needed." The columnist explained his disgusted feeling when he saw the death of children reported in the newspaper, the ones murdered by their parents. He was specifically referring to the seven-month-old Aaden Moreno who was murdered. The columnist made reference to two other children, six years old and seven years old who were murdered by a parent in Connecticut. Mr. Walker, the columnist made reference as well of more than 4,000 children in Connecticut who had to be rescued from their parents last year.

I recently read of two children who were murdered by their mother and placed in a freezer. The other two children saw the mother torturing their siblings. The boy had burns all over his back and he really suffered, and finally succumbed to the torture. The sister was beaten in her head and other areas of her body. The mother then placed both brother and sister's corpse in the freezer. The other children had to pass their siblings every-day in that freezer. They were silent. They were probably afraid of being killed next, so they kept silent. It so happened that for two years no one missed those children until an eviction took place and the bodies were discovered.

There have been several cases where the children and their mothers were murdered. Ladies stay silent for some reason or another. I am aware of the fact that domestic violence numbers are available, but women refuse to make use of them. I cannot and will not judge these domestic violence victims, but I pray that those who are still alive will run for their lives.

There are men who abuse the ladies one minute and bring them a present afterwards to make up. Then the cycle continues. Women sometimes blame themselves when things go wrong in the home. The victim victimizes herself over again. If the man truly loves his wife or girlfriend, he would not abuse her. He would get counselling. I have seen so many women who suffer abuse of some sort. I really feel sad to know that I cannot help.

"Your wife will be like a fruitful grapevine, flourishing within your home.

Your children will be like vigorous young olive trees as they sit around your table." (Psalm 128:3)

"You shall not afflict any widow or fatherless child.

If you afflict them in any way, and they cry at all to me, I will surely hear their cry and my wrath will become hot, and I will kill you with the sword." (Exodus 22:22-24)

Recently I heard a young woman giving account of how she beats her husband. I don't think she was boasting but, instead I think she needed help. It was explained that this present husband is her third husband. One of the earlier husbands went to her mother and explained that it was not working out. A second husband had to go because he equated his wife to a knife and not a wife. She now beats the third if he did not bring home all his paycheck. I can just imagine him with a broken arm or a black eye, and when he is asked about it, he is probably embarrassed to say that his wife did it to him. If he lives in our culture some of us would laugh at him when we know the truth. These grown men have to live with abuse upon abuse. They suffer in silence because of the stigma that it carries if the abuse is revealed.

When homes are deprived of family members, especially children we should expect God's wrath in our land. Someone will want to know if God is really loving, I say resoundingly, yes, He loves our children and our wives that we are destroying by the minute. Our homes should be made safer and God will bless our land.

AT WORK

T he "Me Too" has brought out several secrets in the open that enable some people especially women and young boys to surrender their secrets that they had been silent about.

The workplace is a cruel place where you can be attacked because of your skin color, ethnicity and even because of your qualification. "If you don't work, you don't eat." (2 Thessalonians 3:10).

The Bible is encouraging us to work or else we should not eat. Able bodied men and women should find some form of employment and work or else we should not feed them. I agree with The Apostle Paul, but in our time and days, we take notice of people who are unable to eat after they have worked so hard.

It is very common to hear shootings in the workplace. Someone may have a grudge for someone else, but he slays persons who are innocent. These innocent men and women have had no chance to pick-up their salary or even go home alive from work. They are killed in a cruel act. How sad it is to be minding your own business and producing as you ought, but you are deprived of life.

I know what it is like to have younger women attacking me constantly, and I don't retaliate. Yes, they were young and of different color of skin. In one instance I walked through an empty classroom in order to go to another room, when this young teacher who was attacking me, ordered me not to walk through her classroom again. I responded in a harsh tone instructing her to leave me alone. She raced to the administrator's office and gave some report or other. The administrator sent the social worker to talk to me, and after I explained all that I was enduring, he asked me why I didn't report it.

There was this other young lady, who was working with me and I don't know if the color of my skin, with her being supervised by me was a problem, but she would leave my room and go to other rooms to assist. She lied to at least two parents about me. I was in a meeting with one of the families and my supervisor. I was asked of the child's behavior in class. I gave an honest account, the dad said that that was how he behaved at church and home so they gave him extra activities but he was still overactive. The parent stated in the meeting with the supervisor that the young lady said that the child did nothing.

I will call her Ms. P, (not her name) she began to embarrass me in front of the children and other staff members. One day she did such atrocity in the cafeteria with so many children and adults. I walked out ashamed with my lips closed. I think when we do not respond to verbal abuse, that makes it worse. I am saying this because I know what suffering in silence means. One day Ms. P made a very bad, demeaning, negative comment to the five-year-olds about me. I felt the anger rising within me. I was about to walk out of the room to report it to the administrator, but I know the Holy Spirit held me back. The reason is this, when I feel like how I felt, I talk fast and everything goes in one, so it's a little difficult for someone of another culture to fathom what I am conveying. Many years ago, a teacher informed me to always keep an anecdotal record, so I had a stock of running records. The following day I went to my administrator, who remarked in the end that he had no proof, so I went and got my record, and gave it to him and informed him that it was just written for me.

After my administrator read my report, he summoned her to the office. She returned later and made a remark about if someone who was visiting our building could find her a job. Some people believe that we are weak or that we are fools because we do not respond in the manner in which they know they would. They take advantage of us for no good reason. I have seen good reliable workers who have been attacked constantly with actions and words that reduced the worker to tears.

Several ladies and young women are abused sexually at the workplace. They suffer these abuses because they want to hold a job or certain jobs. They have the ability to seek other employment, but they accept the ones that bring pain. They keep the stories at work a secret because of threat or insecurity. Many unskilled men work for little pay just to provide for their families. They work hard in these dead-end jobs because of different reasons. Some of them are definitely afraid of being discovered because they are undocumented, so they take the abuse. Many of these hardworking men and women cannot complain to the authorities about their long working hours and low paying jobs.

Going to work is as difficult sometimes as living without employment. The two sides of the situation are just as bad. Someone may say, flip a coin, but either side brings suffering in silence. May the Lord help us all.

SUFFERING IN SILENCE
AT CHURCH

· · · · · · · · · · ● ○○○○○○○○ ○ ○ ○

"Let us hold tightly without wavering to the hope we affirm, for God can be trusted to keep His promise. Let us think of ways to motivate one another to acts of love and good works. And let us not neglect our meeting together, as some people do, but encourage one another, especially now that the day of His return is drawing near." (Hebrews 10: 23-25).

The Lord has been gracious to us in inviting us to come and worship. He even informs us of the importance of meeting or congregating together because His return is very close. Someone may question how is it that worshipers have difficulty in church and so they suffer in silence. Only God knows how His children love Him and are committed to Him, yet we are wounded in the church.

Some Christians are wounded spiritually, socially, emotionally and psychologically. There are Christians who carry scars that are unseen to the natural eyes but only God sees the wounds that are inflicted by the church. You get hurt but keep it between you and the Lord or you may tell a trusted friend who will encourage you to keep holding on. It is just a test and if you fail this one, you will have to repeat it. Understandably, there are others who are in the wrong, but they are sailing high and are being lifted up, but it leaves you to wonder what is going on

We occasionally see Christians church-hopping and we wonder why they leave such and such congregation, but they have unbearable pains so that they cannot remain. Everyone knows that the church is a hospital for the wounded, so why does the church constantly inflict wounds?

> "For my dear broken people, I'm heartbroken. I weep, seized by grief.
>
> Are there no healing ointments in Gilead?
>
> Isn't there a doctor in the house?

So why can't something be done to heal and save my dear, dear people?" (Jeremiah 8"21-22)

I think that is widely known of worshippers who have been abused sexually and have kept it a secret for one reason or another. Some have been instructed to keep it quiet and the perpetrator pretends that he is doing ministry and that he is in love with the abused when at the same time he is lying. Women may abuse but I think it is safe to say that 99% of abusers are men.

Let us think of the number of youths who have reported sexual abuse. We have grown men and women who are now exposing "men of the cloth" for the wrongs they have committed. Some of these leaders' actions have been reported to higher authorities who have covered the transgressions under the proverbial rug. Some of the abuses are several decades old but the hurt is as fresh as when the act was committed. I don't think that a million dollars is enough to compensate for these atrocities. I am not implying that they deserve more monetary settlement, I am saying that the pain goes very deep. Many of the males are unable to go to the opposite sex. Some of them are confused.

People are sitting in the church with the proverbial "baggage". They have a heavy weight on their shoulders. When an individual who loves the Lord suffers in church, where can he or she go for solace? I know that we have counselors and therapists, but the church should be the first counselor. God rescues people off drugs and other harmful substances. I remember a friend who did not get outside assistance to cease smoking that bound her for years. The Lord delivered her, and she has been healed for many years and looks younger recently at her 79th birthday party. The church is a hospital, so no one should suffer in silence and belongs to a church. Everyone should be delivered or healed in the church.

My question is, who do you go to when you get hurt? Will you be setting up yourself to be hurt further? If a leader loves the abuser, he/she will not be approached to make right the wrong, especially if she is a Christian bulldozer. We would think that aggressive persons change when they become Christians, but we have to think again. Some of them have not changed and so they strut around with their chest pushed out. May God help and deliver us.

IN AMERICA

• • • • • • • • • ● ○○○○○○○○○○○ ○ ○

It is very pathetic to see the number of young black men who have been killed without a voice. They are slaughtered in their homes and on the streets of America the "Land of the Free." These victims as I think they are, had not put up any resistance to their executioners especially the police officers. These very innocent black young men are not given a chance to speak for themselves. They are shot and killed, and some got the knee that murdered them. There is present day lynching that is somewhat different from former years but lynching just the same.

A young black boy was just jogging and was followed by two murderers, a father and son and they slaughtered this young boy. We were taught that a father trained his son and if this is the way this man trained his son, they both should end up with the electric chair. Wipe the society of that cruel generation. Let it die before there is a grandson to mirror his grandfather and father.

Black men should never have to live in fear, neither on the streets nor in their homes. No black family should be exempt from living in any neighborhood that they can afford. "The earth is the Lord's and everything in it. The world and all its people belong to him." (Psalm 24:1). Blacks, whites and all the other races should enjoy God's earth.

CONCLUSION

I have written this book informing some who are unaware of the pain that others are feeling from their verbal abuses, physical abuses, thoughtlessness, destructive undertones, and unreasonable commands. We sometimes forget that people have feelings and may react when they get hurt.

People need to be respected. We sometimes choose who to love and who to abuse. We should sometimes place ourselves in the other person's place, just switch positions for a while and we will understand why some people respond in the manner they do. Some of us have caused unnecessary tears, pain, disappointments and regrets. We have caused people to lose the trust they once had in us.

I do pray that this book will enlighten us to things, treatment, torture and behaviors that are meted out to others. "Do to others whatever you would like them to do to you. This is the essence of all that is taught in the law of the prophets." (Matthew 7:12)

May we be reminded that Jesus is soon to return. The signs of the times are screaming very loudly, "He is coming soon!" The Bible states: "And the Good News about the Kingdom will be preached throughout the whole world, so that all nations will hear it: and then, finally, the end will come." (Matthew 24:14). Over the years, preachers have quoted this verse, but it really did not take on meaning until recently. We have had preaching in the church, missionaries taking the gospel around the world, evangelists and even underground churches, but we still were unable to fathom what Jesus was really saying.

Our eyes are enlightened with the coming of various types of technologies, and now the Gospel (Good News) is traveling where we are unable to reach physically. Indigenous people who have many languages than they can understand are receiving some message that they understand. God has made it possible that some of His servants, place materials in little machines (as I term them) and one person operates it and shares the message and their lives are changed with what they hear until they acquire more information. The Gospel is travelling far and wide so any day now Jesus can put in His appearance. Let's care for each other and encourage one another as we travel on this pathway. We do need each other. Someone penned this:

> "No man is an island,
> No man stands alone,
> Each man's joy is joy to me,
> Each man's grief's my own,
> We need one another,
> Therefore I defend
> Each man as my brother
> Each man as my friend."
> (author unknown).

Printed in the United States
by Baker & Taylor Publisher Services